OCTOPUS

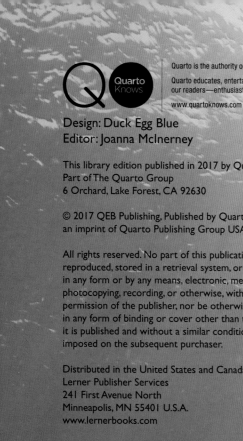

Quarto is the authority on a wide range of topics.

Quarto educates, entertains and enriches the lives of
our readers—enthusiasts and lovers of hands-on living.

www.quartoknows.com

Design: Duck Egg Blue
Editor: Joanna McInerney

This library edition published in 2017 by Quarto Library.,
Part of The Quarto Group
6 Orchard, Lake Forest, CA 92630

Distributed in the United States and Canada by
Lerner Publisher Services
241 First Avenue North
Minneapolis, MN 55401 U.S.A.
www.lernerbooks.com

A CIP record for this book is available from the Library of Congress.

ISBN 978 1 68297 080 5

Printed in China

Contents

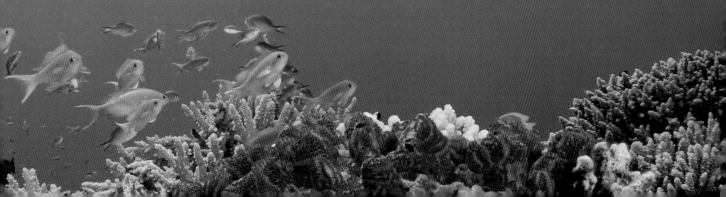

What is an octopus?

Octopuses are amazing ocean animals. They have blue blood, soft bodies, and eight long, bendy **arms**. An octopus belongs to the same family as garden snails and slugs, but it spends its whole life in the sea. Octopuses hunt other animals to eat.

Shape and color

There are no bones inside an octopus's body, so it can squeeze into small places to hide. It can also change its shape and color so hungry animals can't see it. Changing color takes less than one second!

4

That's amazing!

If an octopus loses an arm, it can grow a new one. It uses its arms to hold onto things, and to swim, walk, or crawl on the **seabed**.

Octopuses of the world

There are about 300 different types of octopus. Some of them are no bigger than a fingernail, but others grow bigger than a person. They live all over the world's oceans, from warm water seas to cold water near the **Arctic** and **Antarctic**.

Deep water

Some octopuses, such as dumbo octopuses, live in very deep water. Life in the deepest parts of the oceans is hard because there is not much to eat and it's always cold and dark.

That's amazing!

The biggest octopus in the world is called the Pacific giant octopus. It can grow more than 16 feet (5 m) long! It has a big, round head and its skin is red-brown.

Coral reefs

A coral reef makes a good home for an octopus because there are places to hide from sharks and other big fish. There is plenty of food, too. Reef octopuses live where the sea is **shallow** and warm.

Ocean homes

Most octopuses live near the seabed but they also swim in the open ocean. Octopuses use their arms to move along the seabed. Their arms and **suckers** are very sensitive, so they can feel the rocks and sand, and any animals hiding there.

That's amazing!

Octopuses spend most of the day resting between rocks, but some of them prefer to hide inside seashells. They can even carry the shells with them when they swim!

Laying eggs

Octopuses lay eggs when they are getting old, and are near the end of their lives. Most female octopuses lay their eggs in a dark hiding place, called a **den**, where they take care of them. Some octopuses lay their eggs in empty shells.

Perfect eggs

An octopus egg is about the size of a grain of rice. Large octopuses can lay tens of thousands of eggs at a time, and it can take a mother up to a month to lay all of them.

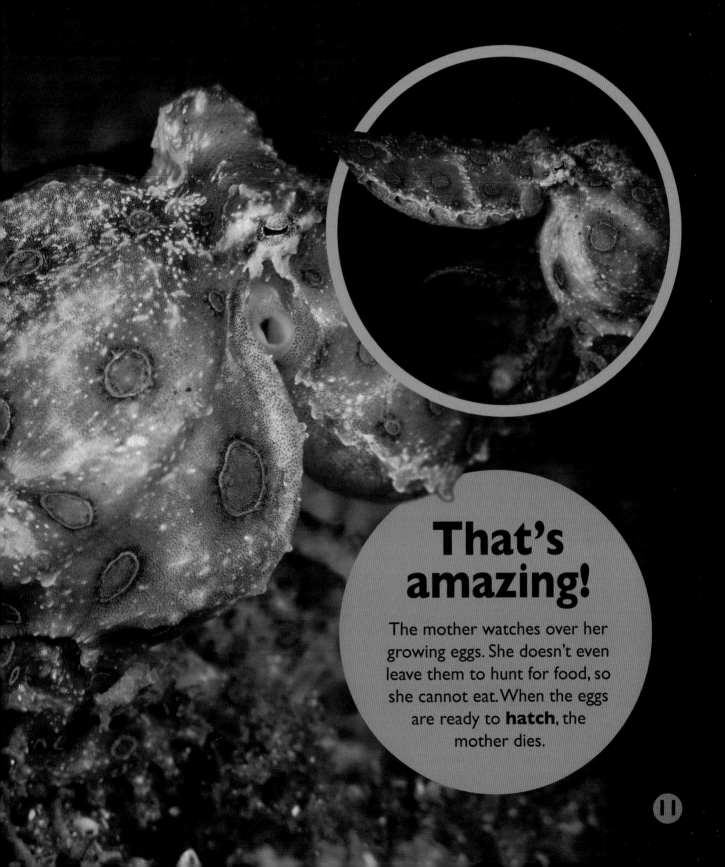

That's amazing!

The mother watches over her growing eggs. She doesn't even leave them to hunt for food, so she cannot eat. When the eggs are ready to **hatch**, the mother dies.

That's amazing!

Most small octopuses live for less than one year! Bigger octopuses can live for three or four years. The way that an animal grows, has babies, and dies is called its life cycle.

Growing up

A baby octopus is called a **hatchling**. It gets washed away from the den and floats near the top of the ocean, along with millions of other tiny animals. It is about one-tenth of an inch (3 mm) long and it is **transparent**.

Top to bottom

Baby octopuses grow quickly. Their little arms grow longer, and they grow suckers on them. As they get heavier the octopuses sink and move towards the bottom of the sea. Now they look like adult octopuses, and have colorful skin.

Feeding

All octopuses—even baby ones—hunt and eat other animals. Animals that hunt are called **predators**. Octopuses hunt at night, when it's easier to creep up on other animals and take them by surprise. Their favorite foods are shellfish, crabs, lobsters, **shrimp**, and fish.

Deadly bite

An octopus grabs its **prey** with its arms. It uses its strong, beaklike mouth to bite and open shells. Octopuses also use **venom** to hurt their prey. Little blue ring octopuses bite with a deadly venom that can kill a human.

That's amazing!

Octopuses have mouths on their undersides! They have tiny teeth for drilling a hole into a shell, so they can get to the soft animal inside.

On the move

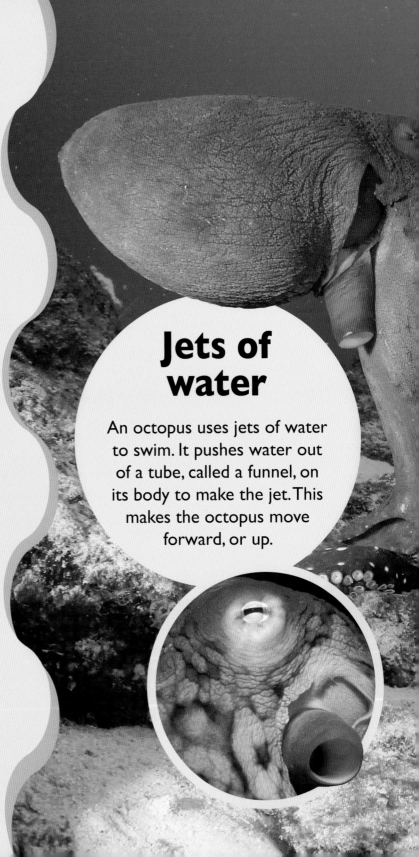

When an octopus moves across the seabed, it almost looks as if it is flowing, not crawling. It uses all its eight arms to slip and slither over rocks, mud, and sand. Most octopuses are not fast movers, but they can swim when they need more speed.

Jets of water

An octopus uses jets of water to swim. It pushes water out of a tube, called a funnel, on its body to make the jet. This makes the octopus move forward, or up.

That's amazing!

Octopuses have three hearts for pumping blood to all their arms. When they swim, their hearts stop beating, so they must take a rest after a long swim and catch their breath!

17

Confusing color

When an octopus is scared, it can change the color of its skin to confuse predators. Two large "eye-spots" can darken on its head, making it look fierce. Octopuses also change the color of their skin and use camouflage to hide.

That's amazing!

Octopuses that live in shallow water blast a cloud of black ink at a predator. The ink turns the water dark, blinding a predator while the octopus flees!

Staying safe

As an octopus swims through the sea, or rests on the seabed, it must watch for predators. There are many animals that may want to hunt and eat an octopus, especially when it is small. An octopus has some clever ways to stay safe.

People and octopuses

Octopuses are interesting animals, because they are smart and can do amazing things. **Scientists** study octopuses to find out more about how they live, how they change color and shape, and how they attack other animals.

Watching octopuses

People **dive** around coral reefs so they can watch octopuses in their natural homes. Some octopuses are kept in **aquariums** so we can learn more about them. They need lots of space, so the aquariums have to be large.

That's amazing!

Octopuses are very smart creatures with huge brains. They have been known to escape from aquariums and find their own way back to the sea!

21

Glossary

Antarctic

The Antarctic is the land at the South Pole.

Aquarium

An aquarium is a large glass tank that is filled with water. Animals that live in water can be kept in aquariums.

Arctic

The Arctic is the area around the North Pole. It is an ocean.

Arms

An octopus's limbs are called arms. It uses them for moving and touching.

Den

This is the home a mother makes where she lays her eggs.

Dive

When people dive they are swimming beneath the surface of the sea.

Hatch

When an egg breaks open it hatches, and the baby animal comes out.

Hatchling

An animal that has just hatched out of an egg is called a hatchling.

Predator

A predator is an animal that hunts other animals to eat.

Prey

An animal that is hunted is called prey.

Scientist

A scientist is a person who works to find out more about something, such as an animal.

Seabed

The floor of the sea or ocean is called the seabed. It is covered in sand, mud, stones, or rocks.

Shallow

Shallow is the opposite of deep.

Shrimp

A shrimp is a small animal with ten legs. It swims in the ocean.

Sucker

A sucker is a round, bowl-shaped area on an octopus's arm. It has muscles for gripping onto things.

Transparent

Something that is transparent is see-through.

Venom

Venom is a poison that an animal makes to defend itself, or to hurt or kill prey.

Index

Picture credits

(t=top, b=bottom, l=left, r=right, fc=front cover, bc=back cover)

Alamy

4-5 Matthew Banks, 6b WaterFrame, 6-7 edward rowland, 7b AF archive, 14b, 14-15 age fotostock, 16br Travis Rowan, 20-21 Reinhard Dirscherl, 21tc Jens Ickler

Nature Picture Library

6r, 15b David Shale, 8bl Alex Mustard, 13bc Nature Production, 16b Georgette Douwma, 20bc David Fleetham

Seapics

5t Stephen Wong, 12-13 John C. Lewis,

Shutterstock

1r, 2cr, 2-3, 16-17 Rich Carey, 1bc, 8-9 Andrea Izzotti, 4b Luke Suen, 4cr littlesam, 9tl Annetje, 9b Iness_la_luz, 12l SergeUWPhoto, 14r kaschibo, 17tr Boris Pamikov, 20r photocritical,